Who is Me

Who is Me

Vivienne Jennings

Copyright © 2011 by Vivienne Jennings.

Library of Congress Control Number: 2011918335
ISBN: Hardcover   978-1-4653-6000-7
              Softcover   978-1-4653-5999-5
              Ebook   978-1-4653-6001-4

All rights reserved. No part of this book may be reproduced or transmitted in any form or by any means, electronic or mechanical, including photocopying, recording, or by any information storage and retrieval system, without permission in writing from the copyright owner.

This book was printed in the United States of America.

To order additional copies of this book, contact:
Xlibris Corporation
0-800-644-6988
www.xlibrispublishing.co.uk
Orders@xlibrispublishing.co.uk

Contents

Acknowledgements 7

Being 9
Minding me 10
Who is me 11
Poetic me 12
Sleeping composition 13
Dawning day 14
Mindful anticipation 15
Complex contradiction 16
Tantalising talent 17
Breaking through 18
Opening up 19
Separation 20
Grains of hope 21
Living transitions 22
Therapeutic break 23
Living Optimism 24
Growing dream 25
Haiku grows 26
Feeling good 27
Regurgitating 28
Hampering 29
Obesity 30
Triathlon 31
Running 32
Elation 34
Learning 35
Fragile future 36

Reorganisation	37
Elsewhere	38
Collaboration	39
Afterwards	40
Citadel Park	41
It's me	42
Underground	43
Remote	44
Changing Earth	45
Soft Centre	46
Birthday celebrations	47
Lust to dust	48
Musicality	49
Melodic meditation	50
My violin	51
Drawing futures	52
One day	53
Property	54
Being a Hoarder	55
Decorating	56
Holiday cottages	57
Notes	58

Acknowledgements

My time working one to one has allowed 'news from self' to emerge and be captured in poetic form. My friends and family have given amazing support and encouragement without which this volume would not exist. Although not named, you all know who you are—Thank You.

Birthing brain
Melting mind
Integrating being
Underlying doing

Done gone home
Setting scene
Stabilised loam
Silting sand

Shifting growing
Following feeding
Feeling famished
Nearly finished

Minding me

How is it that only now
    I have the urge
        To pour out words

How is it that only now
    I am able
        To tell a fable

How is it that only now
    I am feeling
        My inner being

How is it that only now
    I can explore
        My folklore

How is it that only now
    I comprehend
        Where I stand

How is it that only now
    I mind me

Who is me

Pretending to be
    Someone I am not
For so long I forgot
    Who on earth was me

Longing for nourishment
    Controlling conviction
Delighting in excrement
    Creating Constriction

Support for self-development
    Missing envelopment
Emaciated element
    Eternal fulfilment

Celestial serenity
    Cramping obesity
Hovering intensity
    Bewildering eccentricity

Heavens who is me?

Poetic me

Poetic me Musical me
Creativity there to see
Eloquent spontaneity
Unbound by regularity

Time to Space to
Allow words through
Rhythm and rhyme
Making lines mine

Like unlike
Within and against
Resembling the pater
Fighting came later

Sleeping composition

Words flowing in pictures
Meaning created in space
Behind my sleeping eyelids
Stanzas stream fabulous dream

Lines and phrases coming in phases
Visual shapes slotting into place
Remembering anticipation
Capturing the exciting moment

Alarm rudely awakes

Dawning day

Motivation melting away
Exhausting exhilarating
Depressing disconnected day

Leaving losses lounging
Bereft on the tide of life

Amorphous amoeba pulsating
Swallowing digesting regurgitating

Mournful munching metamorphosis
Sickening somnolence serving

Creativity crushed incessantly
Slithering sliding spontaneity

Hoping helping hindering
Loving lurching lingering
Along the tortuous way

Dawning day

Mindful anticipation

Mighty manly mindfulness
Enabling emerging consciousness
Freeing flying eternity
Reaching out for maternity

Sharing singing synthesising
Training travelling terrorising
Colourful optimism
Flowering prism

Rotating rainbow
Flow ideas flow
Off to the wind
For others to find

Catching connecting caring
Bridging bowling baring
Soulful serene syncopation
Androgynous anticipation

Complex contradiction

Explosion of emotion
Controlling crumbling contortion
Fragility of feeling
Living lumbering learning

Creating consternation
Ruts rules regulation
Draining determination
Frying frustration

Reigning in free spirit
Trembling toying tacit
Silent erosion
Complex contradiction

Tantalising talent

Tramlined tyranny totally torrential
Parental perambulation precluding potential
Cosseting conditional currency
Framing formulating fluency

Brave bellowing bosom
Manipulating metal microcosm
Finding friendly forays
Struggling shifting stays

Watery wallowing wonderings
Hooting hopping hoverings
Fathoming feathering refrain
Beaming booming brain

Combining combing coming
Hallowed hopeful homing
Cathartic creative contemplation
Tossing transitional temptation

Unforeseen undulating urge
Enduring emissaries emerge
Teasing tantalising talent
Personally potent

Breaking through

Feelings frying in the furnace
Emerging towards the surface
Scrambling hard for recognition
Affect alongside cognition

Elemental empathy energising
Embryonic ideas synthesising
Cooling calming contortions
Finding optimum proportions

Balancing mind and matter
Positioned in order to flatter
Alignment of postural catch
Confidence growing to match

Opening up

Opening up to criticism and rejection
Opportunities for learning and reflection
Analysis digs beneath the surface
Growth goes at an accelerating pace

Comfortable in the limelight
Needing incredible insight
Whilst self remains vulnerable
Support is immeasurable

Separation

Just be my wife
There is my life
I want to leave
I'm left to grieve

Going up North
What am I worth
Another girl
Heavens a whirl

Work together
Vows forever
Different aim
Break up in shame

Lack of respect
Want to defect
So . . . my soul mate
That is our fate

You are alright
I'm left to fight
Years will go by
But I will try

Grains of hope

Living loving losing
Scything sapping spoiling
Direction from the piper's purse
For better or for worse

Dictating demeaning disbelief
Love hate anger and grief
Acceptance giving way to mourning
Patient metamorphic spawning

Framing fumbling fenestration
Blowing icy penetration
Contemplating adjustments
Hollering hunger ferments

Searching softening spirituality
Nurturing nascent musicality
Outside inside growing stronger
Elasticity purposefully longer

Mending mind bereft of meaning
Waiting wistful wishing weaning
Leaving behind the skeins of rope
Gently garnering grains of hope.

Living transitions

Living transitions
Transcend partitions
Boundaries galore
Hold my stuff in store

Stimulating change
May feel somewhat strange
But leaving behind
The life I did find

Is hard to plan for
I need a mentor
Special sustenance
Plan for maintenance

Avoiding relapse
I must not collapse
So all these factors
Are my creator

Now moving forward
Always on my guard
Scaffolding in place
I can see my face

Therapeutic break

Intermittent tearfulness struggles to the surface
Supporting frameworks disappear into the abyss

Time for reflection and restoration
Perhaps even to acknowledge sensation

Numbers, words, music, and pictures
Let them not suffer from constrictures

How then to maximise connections
Listen and share multiple reflections

Vivienne is talking to Vivienne
I have to listen

Living Optimism

Deeply infantile urges
Bubbling beneath the surface
Carefully self emerges
Caressing creative space

Clarifying reflections
Dance playfully in the sun
Spontaneous translations
Meaningful webs to be spun

Sparkling insights are forming
Tantalising mountain climbs
Flowing fantasies racing
Candles flickering in mines

Dense nourishing dialogues
Acting to release feelings
This is only the prologue
Creating fruitful peelings

Releasing tight compression
Lighting colourful prism
Powering motivation
Brighter living optimism

Growing dream

Wondering what the future will hold
As changes take effect
Openings encourage me to be bold
As I ponder which pathway to select

Life's journey is not always simple
Misleading rose-coloured spectacles
Mountains created from a pimple
Hurdles, bars, and conspiring obstacles

Where is my dream
Without it I cannot grow
The cat may have the cream
But my thoughts flow

Haiku grows

Seeing me clearly
Is essentially helpful
As I am growing

Feeling good

Health is not just absence of disease
With oneself there must be ease
Having genetic benefaction
Doesn't preclude the need for action

Environmental considerations
Create conducive conditions
For realisation of potential
Many factors are essential

Regularly being active
Family and others supportive
A sense of security
Enhances our capacity

Feelings of satisfaction
Not lured by distraction
Emanate from busyness
From which there is success

Years are for living
Life for creating
Moments of pure bliss
Would not go amiss

Regurgitating

Anorexic restriction bulimic regurgitation
Rhythmical rhyming in poetic translation
Consciousness unfurling from deep within
Gaining and losing becoming thin

Creative interplay providing foundation
Fathoming meaning amidst such commotion
Feelings connecting deeply emerging
Losing and gaining abundantly strengthening

Hampering

Smothered presentation
Blocking alimentation
Sinews strained
Completely drained

Weighty reluctance
Hampering performance
Sapping energy
Missing synergy

Receding impediment
Inviting nourishment
Releasing brake
Dancing overtake

Essential synthesis
Pupating chrysalis
Savour celebration
Open presentation

Obesity

Creeping adipose extends the bulge
Inevitable when tempted to indulge
Food that compensates for feeling
Sending mind and body reeling

Emotions crushed by comfort eating
Are hard to balance by sweating
Culture obstructs expression of fears
Locking in essential tears

Success, security and satisfaction
Key feelings requiring articulation
Liberating energy for physical activity
Warding off creeping obesity

Smoothly through the water swimming
Aquatic weed and fishes brimming
Catch to propel body over the barrel
Enrobed in stretchy neoprene apparel

Wrestling and dripping
Speedily stripping
Negotiating the verge
From transition emerge

Lycra clad cycling and pedalling
Driving the intent of medalling
Cornering efficiently exit acceleration
Focusing intently on power application

Approaching, de-shoeing
Leaping dismounting
Steering the bike
No mean hike

Rhythmical motion exiting to run
Stay relaxed enjoy the fun
One goes much faster if smiling
Pacing efforts to realistic miling

Hydration, nutrition and training
Are key to optimal performing
Deciding the finishing positions
Swim, cycle, run and transitions

Running

Cadence smoothly flowing
Shoulders relaxed and swinging
Forehead smooth and wide
As feet get into their stride

Core engages positively
Pace rises incrementally
Power application gets stronger
Breathing and pumping go faster

Skimming over the ground
There is hardly a sound
Mid foot strike is light
But quads are yelling tight

Endurance not a sprinter
But getting fitter
Speed play Fartlek
Sounds rude, oh heck

Aerobic capacity
Prepares for intensity
Long slow distance
Rewards persistence

LSD, speed and highs
Hamstrings and thighs
The runner's creed
To increase speed

No need for a pill
Flying up the hill
Primes endorphins
But mind your shins

Run jog walk
Can you talk
Build gradually
Enjoy eternally

Elation

Quietened elation
Begging to be released
Allow celebration
Feel satisfaction

Enjoying the pleasure
Of moments to treasure
Now time for some rest
Having done your best

Memories can play tricks
Don't dream of perfection
Lest your mind delivers kicks
And steels the jubilation

Learning

Ruminating reflections
Reflexive reactions

Harvesting resources
Open access courses

Questioning quotations
Risky sensations

Pulsating dialogue
Developing pedagogue

Fragile future

What is the point
I feel like giving up
I'm in the wrong place
At the wrong time

Research intensity
Teaching insensitivity
Play the game
Not the same

Learning and teaching
Is far reaching
Transforming lives
'Leadership' thrives

Yet here am I
Cast out to graze
Is it the right time
The right place?

Roller coaster ride
Mixed feelings inside
Fragile future
Retiring allure

Reorganisation

What follows Subject Centres?
Where will academics turn?
Electronic enhancement enters
Connected networks churn

Supporting learning
Developing teaching
Assessing capability
Promising employability

Discipline dialogue cacophony
Centralised within the Academy
Values and ethos, people and spin
Opening doors will beckon within

Elsewhere

Cutting the atmosphere with a knife
Reminded us that there is more to life
Than batting our heads against a wall

Cooperating and collaborating
In enhancing learning
Creating common visions for all

Feedback feeding forward
Future facing forays
Discipline driven activities
Engaging dialogue and debates

Following constructive guidelines
To manage change
In learning and teaching
Is a goal for beaming

Collaboration

Conceptual growing
Information flowing
Active participation
Excited transformation

Deeply involving
Collaborative working
Together achieving
Facilitated learning

Surpassing outcomes
Making a difference
Rigorous researching
Practical theorising

Challenging complexity
Contact and chaos
Innovative simplicity
Interprofessionality

#

Reflections captured for two years post
Another European city prepares to host
Gathering to share ideas and developments
Conceptual alongside social moments

Exhilaration emerging after conference
Time to explore the city's confluence
Aboard a boat plying the water
A tourist taking opportunities on offer

Bells, beers and restaurants
Museums, music and festivals
Wandering cobbled back street
Chocolate and park discovered by feet

Thoughts revolving in my brain
Urged on by imminent train
Journeying through the countryside
Contemplation casts work aside.

Citadel Park

Tranquil surroundings
Statues arise from water
Distant traffic moans
Ducks paddle and wander

Student picnic and chatter
Geese approach the spread
Youngsters move away
Birds lose interest and stay

Raucous interruptions
Disturb the contemplations
Again everything settles
My mind is free to roam

Warmth invades us all
A passing runner flows
Now to find the station
Wake up . . . a reality call

It's me

Rolling leaning motion
Catching musical beats
Drinking tidal waves
Sharing conversations

Hello it's me
The train is late
Take away great
See you soon

Soporific lull
Jolting awake
Shoot off
Just in time

Settling back along the line
Rhythmic salutations hiss
Crackling clarity erupts
Droplets dribble sideways

Reach to slide the window
Grapple for the handle
Wait; don't go I need to leave
Here . . . Now

Underground

Peas in a pod we are not
This underground lot
Free newspapers and earphones
Save us from smart phones

Shall I make eye contact
Or even start a chat
Read the ads and notices
While listening to hysterics

Rattling through the tunnel
Mopping sweaty flannel
Spill out across the gap
Round people in a flap

Avoiding the contractors
Moving up escalators
Standing on the right
Climbing to the light

Remote

Mobile stops perambulation
As the need for conversation
Overtakes spatial awareness
Obstructing others' progress

Lives are so important
There is no spare moment
To stand or sit or think
Is life that close to the brink?

Notice when we listen
Eyes begin to glisten
Nurturing connection
Living protection

Changing Earth

Environmental pedagogy
Essential sustainability
Changing organisations
Evolving solutions

Community curricula
Campus culture
Travelling arriving
Collaborating sharing

Learners engaged
Evaluation managed
Leaders satisfied
Futures dignified

Soft Centre

The nascent day dawns
We all shed a tear
A small person yawns
Celebrate our year

Many decades on
Our baby conceives
Where have the years gone
Buy chocolate leaves

Decorate the cake
Find them a present
Picnic by the lake
A beautiful scent

Resembling beetle
Hard shell soft centre
So many people
Joining together

Friendship memories
Jelly and ice cream
More and more babies
Completing the dream

Birthday celebrations

Annual Birthday Celebrations
Dent Enduring Felicitations

Growing Hopefulness Imbibing
Joyful Kindliness Lurking

Mellow Notional Opening
Present Quota Reviewing

Sifting Teasing Undulations
Vibrant Willowing Xpressions

Yonder Zimmer Allowing
Bouncing Childlike Dreaming

Enriching Fitness Gruel
Hilly Inclining Jewel

Kindles Loving Motion
Never Offered Potion

Quoting Reminiscent Somnolence
Trembling Uncertain Violence

Welcome Xciting
Youthful Zeal

Lust to dust

Celebrating birthing
Baby emerging
Wrinkly and bald

Lacking dentition
What an apparition
Genetic definition
Phenotypic manifestation

Adolescent psychology
Childhood Gerontology
Lacking dentition
Wrinkly and bald

Musicality

Lifting deep depression
Building on a succession

Of searches for causes
Interspersed with pauses

Giving time for experiments
Selecting the best elements

To help with expression
And promote relaxation

Life makes more sense
Now that I'm not so tense

Strengthening connections
Facilitating introspections

Blossoming spirituality
Motivating musicality

Melodic meditation

Mindful melodic meditation
Serene soothing syncopation
Bemusing baffling brilliance
Releasing responsive resonance

Freeing feminine fantasies
Illuminating irregular intricacies
Trembling tempestuous temperament
Illusive imploring instrument

Playing pianissimo pizzicato
Startling symphonic staccato
Fragile future fermenting
Majestic musical meaning

My violin

Harbouring fantasies of being melodic
But practising is somewhat spasmodic
Notes don't quite fall into place anymore
Friends and family I don't want to bore

My childhood instrument a violin
(Though there's the intrigue of a mandolin)
Rhythmical bowing smoothly up and down
Orchestral practice creating a frown

Capable of playing a concerto
Rehearsals require careful staccato
Sharps and flats demand full dexterity
More playing improves flexibility

Gradually proficiency returns
Persistence lights the inner fire that burns
Together the sounds start to resonate
Mindful melodies move and mediate

Drawing futures

Upside down drawing
Really makes me think
About what I am seeing
It created a small chink

In my overall attitudes
That caused a negative reaction
Derived from unwanted platitudes
As my pencil attempted action

My drawings are not artistic
Though helped with frame and grid
May be I am just pessimistic
Because of what happened as a kid

I've drawn my hand
In various positions
Now I can expand
As multiple transitions

Allow sufficient space
To dream and create
Skills are not yet ace
But I'm going through the gate

One day

Eyes and hands might coordinate
When trying to create
Sometime in the future
Some kind of a picture

On paper or canvas
Of person or a vase
Will I draw or paint
Either and I'll faint

Whatever form of expression
It will make an impression
And may even have a frame
If friends came

No image yet exists
Though the desire persists
One day
I'll play

Property

Lacking communication
Nearing completion
Spelling errors remain
Legalese still to explain

Buyer and seller are strong
Why does it take so long
More questions raise the fee
Transferor to transferee

Anger and frustration simmer
Surrounds become dimmer
Finance shifts from spot to spot
Scaffolding moves around the plot

Considerable renovation
Desiring careful decoration
Driving me insane
Bring out the champagne.

Being a Hoarder

Habitual hoarding
Is not rewarding
When piles of clutter
Cause me to fret and mutter

'It might come in useful one day'
But all this stuff inhibits play
Family habits are hard to break
Trinkets are probably fake

Books, clothes and many a bowl
Bursting cupboards and shelves cajole
Me into action, well sometimes
When visitors come from sunnier climes

There is a sense of liberation
When at last I find the motivation
To de-clutter and tidy up
Though there is the odd hiccup

Of course

Decorating

"I wish I hadn't taken the job on"
Is it that hard to paint behind a pipe?
Into the corners, keep windows opening
Decorator please pay attention to detail

I don't want perfection
Though I would like some satisfaction
For underlying durability
As well as aesthetically

I know I have high standards
And expect others to agree
If only I were here
Then you might adhere

Forgive me for criticising
I really prefer praising
But when tiredness and stress prevail
You may think I'm beyond the pale

Holiday cottages

The sadness of selling the barn
Is countered by the yarn
Of creating sustainable sutures
For family focused futures

Boundaries are established
Drains are carefully swished
Services run through trenches
Courtyard garden fences

Land is dug and flattened
Roofs are stripped and battened
Walls of carboniferous limestone
Inside outside flagstone

Outbuildings to be conserved
Ancient features are preserved
Cast iron hoppers and gutters
Observe St George that flutters

Autumn fern and golden umber
Create a peaceful place to slumber
Or exercise on the levels
And return to party revels

Holiday accommodations
Aim to meet your expectations

Notes

Notes

Notes

Notes

Notes

Notes

Lightning Source UK Ltd.
Milton Keynes UK
UKOW050213201211

184083UK00001B/139/P